Aliens Stole My Dog

Ian Whybrow

illustrated by Tony Ross

Hodder
Children's
Books

a division of Hodder Headline Limited

For Toby Alexander Savill

Text copyright © 2000 by Ian Whybrow
Illustrations copyright © 2000 by Tony Ross

First published in Great Britain in 2000
by Hodder Children's Books

The rights of Ian Whybrow and Tony Ross to be identified as the Author and Illustrator
of the Work respectively have been asserted by them in accordance with the Copyright,
Designs and Patents Act 1988.

10 9 8 7 6 5 4 3 2 1

A Catalogue record for this book is available from the British Library.

ISBN 0340 77893 8

Printed and bound in Great Britain by
Guernsey Press Ltd, Guernsey, Channel Islands

Hodder Children's Books
A Division of Hodder Headline Limited
338 Euston Road
London NW1 3BH

Stand By to Beam

David found the CD-rom in the
playground as he was going home
from school on Friday. He'd been
feeding the snails and cleaning the
glass in the
vivarium,
so he was
last to go as
usual. There
was nobody
else about.

Never mind, he would wait till Monday and take it into Lost Property then. There was no harm in trying it out in the meantime, he thought.

As he turned into Beech Avenue, he was hit by a very nasty smell. It came from the old dump that was on the other side of the bypass. When the wind blew from the north-west, you often had to hold your nose. His dad owned a flower shop and was always complaining about it.

He said it drove customers away from the high street. He and the other local shopkeepers would soon be ruined.

David pressed his hanky to his nose and hurried home. He couldn't wait to get up to his room. He dashed straight to his Game-station  and loaded the CD-rom.

He had dozens of different games, but none of them seemed as real as this one. He was a pilot on a very fast spaceship, looking through the cockpit window.

At first he rushed along deep in space, with stars and asteroids and planets flashing by. In no time at all he zoomed past the moon and headed straight for Earth.

Europe came rushing towards him, then England. And then! Before he knew it he was hovering over Elmfield, the little town where he lived. There was the main shopping street, Arkwright Road. Amazing!

Next, two pointy things appeared in the middle of the screen. One was marked "blaster" and the other "beam upper". David pressed the right button on his joystick. Blam! The blaster fired and the litter box outside the chemist's shop glowed red-hot, then melted into a puddle of plastic.

"Wow!" gasped David. He had been sitting on that litter box only yesterday.

Then, as the spaceship drifted down Arkwright Road, the beam upper started to point all by itself. It pointed at the window of chemist's shop, then at Grove's the butcher, then at the Oxfam shop, then at a lamppost. David's heart began to beat like a drum.

He knew that the next shop in the row, the one after the post office, was his dad's flower shop. He saw Dad come out to water the buckets of flowers outside on the pavement.

At that moment, the joystick vibrated in David's hand. He felt it tug. The words **STAND BY TO BEAM** appeared on the screen and David suddenly found to his horror that the beam upper was directed straight at . . . his dad!

"Look out, Dad!" he yelled.

With all his strength, David jerked the joystick to the left. The beam upper swung so that it pointed just to one side of Dad.

Dad's roses came closer and closer until the screen was filled with a single

rose. On one of the petals, a greenfly twitched and twisted.

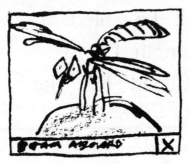

Close up, it looked like some sort of prehistoric monster.

The words **BEAM ABOARD!** lit up on the screen. David pressed the fire button to see what would happen.

10

A ray shot out from the beam

upper, the insect turned blue, then violet, then – *Tzzz!* – it was gone. The

joystick gave a little shudder.

EARTHLIFE SAMPLE STORED!
flashed the words on the screen.
David's jaw dropped. What on Earth
did that mean? he wondered.

Three Worrying Things

It was Sunday morning. Dad was raking up leaves in the garden. David's dog, Hairy Spice, was helping. Mum was in the kitchen, cooking lunch.

David was upstairs in his bedroom playing on his Gamestation. By now, he was a whizz at the new game.

He couldn't get enough of
gliding over the streets and fields
and factories of Elmfield, then
rocketing deep into space. Beaming
up was great, too. His aim was
getting really good
and he'd fished up
all sorts of things.

His cleverest
thing was zapping
the bike out from
under the large
policeman who
was riding it. And
he lifted the cod and chips
right off the newspaper from Roy
Lewis, the bully who was always
pinching his stuff.

Then there was blasting – that was fantastic! But just after he had blasted an old mattress and a fridge that somebody had dumped on the tow-path beside the canal, his fun was interrupted by a yell from downstairs. It was Mum.

"David! David! Where is that boy?"

It was at that exact moment that David noticed three worrying things . . .

The smell of burning coming from downstairs.

The sound of a tornado.

The alien spacecraft that was hovering over the back garden.

David dropped the joystick and stared open-mouthed out of the window. He rubbed his eyes – but it was true! The spaceship was twice as big as the garden shed and shaped like a big steam iron, only with two pointy things sticking out of the front.

David thought the pointy things seemed awfully familiar. And now they were aiming right at his dad! Dad had his back to the spaceship. Hadn't he seen it yet? Hadn't he even *heard* it?

David held his breath and trembled. Before he could scream a warning, David saw the blaster aim at the kitchen and the beam upper pointing straight at him! David threw himself down on to his bedroom floor and tried to scramble under one of his curtains.

He heard a loud BLAM! from downstairs, and at the same time, a pink ray flashed out from the spaceship. It beamed through the window over David's head and bounced round the walls. Vbbb! Vbbb! Vbbb! It bounced off the window frame and settled not on him, but on the Gamestation.

David gasped as it lifted the CD-rom into the air. It went blue, then violet, then – *Tzzz!* – it skimmed once round the room like a silver frisbee before being pulled at lightning speed on board the spaceship.

What had happened? David
sat dazed with shock, until the
sound of Mum's shouting snapped
him to attention.

"David! Will you get down here
and open the back door for me! I've
got my hands full!"

He raced down the stairs three at
a time. The kitchen was full of black
smoke. Mum was standing in the
middle of it, coughing. She had her
oven gloves on and she was holding
a roasting tin that contained
the black, scorched remains
of a chicken, roast
potatoes and
parsnips, David's
favourite.

"I can't understand what happened!" Mum shouted. "I turned my back just to set the table and –

 whoosh! The oven door burst open and started spewing smoke!

Well, it's ruined now. Absolutely ruined. There's nothing for it but to throw it outside in the bin."

"I shouldn't go into the garden if I were you, Mum." He didn't want her in the firing line as well as Dad. He ran between her and the back door.

"Don't be ridiculous, David! I've got to get rid of this mess! Mind out of the way," she snapped.

David was trembling, but Mum didn't seem to notice. "Mum," David warned in a voice that was barely a whisper. "There's . . . something out there."

But Mum wasn't listening. She pushed past David and opened the door. Nervously, David followed her outside.

Aliens Stole My Dog!

The spaceship had landed. David watched it squatting on the lawn, glowing. Like a cat from outer space, ready to pounce.

There were flattened daffodils and scattered tulip petals everywhere.

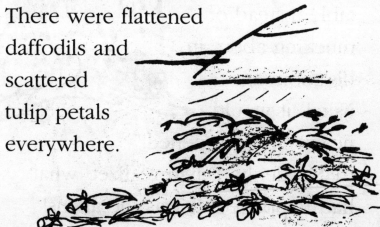

Then David remembered the
three strange things that had
happened at once. One of them had
been the sound of a tornado . . .

"Just look what's happened to
the dinner!" Mum complained to
Dad, putting the hot roasting tin
down on the path. "I told him
I was busy ironing.
If only he'd come
down and laid the
table instead of
mucking about in
his room as
usual, it would
never have happened!"

Suddenly, David realized what
had happened. It was the aliens!

They'd zapped it!

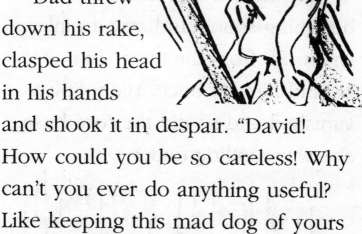

Dad threw down his rake, clasped his head in his hands and shook it in despair. "David! How could you be so careless! Why can't you ever do anything useful? Like keeping this mad dog of yours

from getting in my way. I only tidied this garden up yesterday and look at the state of it! Just look! She's a disgrace!"

"You've got it all wrong," insisted David. "Hairy Spice is innocent!"

Just then, David heard a humming sound and saw a pink ray shoot out from the alien ship behind him. At once, Hairy Spice vanished and so did the rose bush she was rootling under.

"Dad! Help! Did you see that? Aliens stole my beautiful dog!" yelled David.

Mum said, "Where *is* the little pest? Don't say it's got under the gate again! Probably off ruining someone else's garden."

David stood there, completely speechless. By now it was obvious that neither Mum nor Dad could see the alien spacecraft. In fact, Dad walked straight through it, just as if it were made of cloud, and went to help Mum by lifting the dustbin lid, so that she could empty the burnt roast dinner into it.

"What a day! As if I haven't got enough to worry about, what with the smell from the dump ruining my business! And now I've got nothing to look forward to for my Sunday dinner except beans on toast," Dad complained.

"Yes, and I've a jolly good mind to make David clean the oven. It's absolutely filthy – black as soot!" grumbled Mum.

"I hope that burnt food isn't going to set fire to the rubbish," Dad snapped. "That's the last thing I need – having the fire brigade stamping all over my lawn!"

"That's it! Call the fire brigade, Dad," said David. "Or maybe call the army."

"Stop being ridiculous and look for that dog," said Dad. "And don't come back in till you've found her."

Dad opened the back door and followed Mum into the house. The door slammed, leaving David alone with the spaceship.

I've had it now, David thought.
He took a deep breath, closed his
eyes, and expected at any moment
to get zapped. Slowly, trying not to
draw attention to himself, he put his
arms over his ears and curled into a
ball. Nothing happened. He sneaked
a peep through his fingers. The
spaceship was there, but still.

Everything was
completely still.
Then one of the
daffodils that lay
flattened by the wind
stood up and spoke to him.
"Stand by to come on
board!" it
commanded.

David Meets the Klergs

It is a very shocking thing to be spoken to by a daffodil. Even after all the strange things that had happened so far, David was completely stunned by it, but luckily, he managed to stop himself fainting and to put up his hands.

"I surrender!" he cried. Then he
half crawled, half rolled up to the
daffodil and spoke into the trumpet
as if it were an old-fashioned
telephone. Nervously, he said, "My
name is David Gasper. I come in
peace. Please don't zap me." He
waited for a few seconds. Nothing
happened, so he said, "Over."

The voice that came from the
flower was weird. It was deep and
sounded like somebody blowing
through a straw in a milkshake.

"Greetings, David Gasper," it burbled. "I come from the planet Klerg. I am the Commander of the spacecraft *Earthlife Explorer.* Congratulations. You have passed our tests. We have chosen you to travel with us to see our Leader on the other side of Universe 7."

"T-t-tests? What tests have I passed?" stuttered David.

"Firstly, you have shown yourself to be an excellent space pilot," burbled the Klerg Commander. "You have shown that you know this part of Earth well. So you have passed the Earthguide test. Also, you are an expert blaster and beam upper."

David said, "Do you mean that the CD-rom I found wasn't just a game? Do you mean it was a mini spaceship?"

The Commander explained that the "CD-rom" was in fact a VTP or Virtual Training Program, a small pod sent by the mother-ship – the ship that was now on David's lawn. It had now returned to its dock.

"When you picked up the CD-rom in the playground," the Commander went on, "you put your fingerprints on it. Those fingerprints contained tiny traces of your DNA.

This allowed a computer on the mother-ship to set up a link with

the seeing and hearing parts of your brain. But we can communicate only with you. Nobody else can hear or see us."

It was just as David had suspected.

The Commander continued, "We are interested in the samples of Earthlife that you chose to collect. They are all safe now with us. Like that small green monster with six legs."

It was the greenfly that he'd
beamed up on Friday. David tried to
remember what he had beamed up
since . . . that policeman's bike, the
fish and chips . . . then there was
Mrs Lewis's washing,
some traffic cones,
a phone box, a
shopping trolley, a
pair of false teeth
. . . Oh yes, and a
cow-pat. Oh dear.
What a good thing he hadn't
beamed up any people.

Just then, the spaceship glowed
a very angry purple. The pink ray
that David knew so well flicked out
and glowed all round him.

"Now, that is enough talk. Our Leader's patience will be running out! Stand by now for beaming up!" bubbled the Commander.

"I'm not going in there!" shouted David, putting up his fists bravely, like a little boxer (although he was still very scared).

"It is useless to try to resist!" threatened the Commander. "Remember that we can blast you as we blasted that heat-ray you aimed at us."

"That wasn't a heat-ray! That was the oven!" yelled David.

But it was no use. The Klerg
Commander's voice was like
underwater thunder.

"David Gasper, I must tell you
that if you do not obey, some of the
life forms that we have captured
already will be very disappointed.
We may have to destroy them,
starting with your sister!"

Kidnapped!

"Sister?" stammered David. "What do you mean? I haven't got a sister."

"Of course you have!" said the Klerg Commander. "I will describe her. Her skin is covered all over with grass, like you have on the hard round thing on top of your body. She speaks a different language but our computer has translated it like this, 'Me fetch stick. Me roll over. Me want doggy dins.

Me hear brother call, *Heel, girl!* Me follow. He smell nice.'"

"Hairy Spice!" said David. A picture of her bewildered face leapt into his mind. He sighed. "She hates being on her own. I've got to get her back! What have you done with her?"

"We have shrunk the life-forms. They are stored in spacetubes in our on-board lab," said the Commander.

"*They*?" asked David. "Who else have you kidnapped?"

"We have one loud, fierce female in yellow armour with a long metal weapon. She says you go slowly past her nearly every day and she talks to you. Also, a large adult male Number 9 with no grass on his round part. He is your commander. He carries his command-giver on a string around his neck. It is very loud. His inner skin is red. His outer body is a hard blue shell."

David racked his brains to think who these extraordinary people could be.

He thought and
thought. Pictures
of female knights
and bossy crabs
came into his
mind. Who had
disappeared lately?
Only Mr Giles, his class teacher. He
had been away from school since
Wednesday. Everybody said he
caught a cold. And serve him right
for making them play football in the
rain and the wind!

Football! Wind? Of course! The last time David had seen Mr Giles, he was sitting in his blue Mini, sheltering from the weather while David and the other players had to run for it into the changing rooms! The Klergs must have beamed him up in his car! The Mini was his hard blue shell! The wind was caused by the thrusters on the Klerg spaceship.

It was the same force that had
flattened his dad's
flowers. And what did Mr
Giles wear when he
was refereeing? A red
tracksuit. That was the
inner skin the
Commander
mentioned.

And Mr Giles was always
blowing his whistle.
"Command-giver" was a
good word for it. He
fancied himself as a striker, too,
which why he always wore
Number 9! Oh dear. Next time he
blew his command-giver it would
be in another universe!

 It didn't take much time after that to work out that the fierce female in the yellow armour with the long metal weapon was the grumpy Lollipop Lady who looked after the crossing outside St Hilda's School. She was always shouting at him to stop daydreaming and get a move on.

Still, no matter how much Mr Giles and the Lollipop Lady got on his nerves, David realized that a lot of people were going to be very upset if they disappeared into outer space. He had to act fast.

Suddenly he felt as if he were being grabbed by a strong hand and ripped from the lawn into the air. In a split second, he found himself on the flight deck of the Klerg spaceship, standing in a small transparent chamber, looking at some very strange creatures from outer space.

Welcome, Earthlife Guide!

The biggest one must be the
Commander, David thought. He
switched between being orange with
green lumps like warts, and being
green with orange warty lumps. He
had eyes on stalks and instead of
arms or legs, he had long strands
like electric cables coming out of his
body. Some were plugged into the
flight control panel and one of them
gripped one of the twin joysticks.

He moved by rotating his skin like the chain-wheels on a Caterpillar tractor. In this way, he rolled towards David and released him from the beam upper chamber.

"Welcome, Earthlife Guide," he gargled. "Allow me to introduce you to my crew."

David looked around and saw rows of screens and flashing instruments.

In front of them, plugged into machines, sat several other creatures that glowed either orange or green.

They looked exactly the same as the Commander but only about the size of one of his lumps. This was because they *were* his lumps. He explained how he could break a lump off himself and pop it into the cloning chamber to make a mini-version of himself.

"Sunshield!" he called and one of the mini-aliens unrolled itself like a roller blind in front of a porthole.

"Temperature control!" he said, and two others spun like rotors, creating a nice breeze. "Starmap!" gurgled the Commander and another little blob turned itself into a model of the solar system. "Back to me, Number 6!" he said finally, and one of them threw himself at him like a snowball and became a green lump once more.

At that moment, something else caught David's eye through the flightdeck window.

The paper boy was strolling up the path towards his house, whistling, late as usual. One of the Commander's tentacles flashed towards the fire button on the beam upper.

"No!" yelled David. "Leave him!"

The Commander was very angry at being interrupted, but he didn't press the button. Instead, he glowed hotly and said to David. "It is unwise to say no to me. But we have only a little time left.

"So listen carefully to your orders. It is up to you now to find three samples of Earthlife that will please our Leader. If you do well, we shall release you and go in peace. If you fail, we shall destroy your planet! Take the controls!"

The Klergs Learn How to Have Fun

What a responsibility for
Commander Gasper of *Earthlife
Explorer*! He took a deep breath
before he set off on the most
important mission of his life: to save
the world and rescue his teacher, a
lollipop lady and his pet dog. But
what on Earth should he choose?

"Hold tight!" he yelled and hit
the "maximum thrust" button. What
a feeling!

Scared as he was, David felt he was playing the most exciting game of his life. His mum and dad were always complaining about the amount of time he spent mucking about on his Gamestation and his computer. But all that practice was going to come in handy.

"First, I shall show you something we call fun," he shouted.

"Observe and stand by to copy, crew!" ordered the Commander. David dropped the ship to ground level in a dive that took his breath away. He whizzed under bridges and through railway tunnels and hopped over hedges and houses until he came to the park.

He zigzagged slowly across it,
pointing out to the aliens all the
special places like tree-houses and
dens; swings and see-saws and
slides; and the good skateboard
places and the secret hidy-holes.
The Commander was very impressed.

"Fun is good," he agreed. "Copy,
crew!" The little Klergs had a brilliant
time playing different games.

"Fun copied and stored, Commander!" trilled the one who had become a roundabout. Then he spun round really fast until he almost disappeared. When he stopped, he was his old shape again. The rest of the crew followed his example, turning into cowboys or cops or see-saws or skateboards for a second before returning to their normal shape.

David pulled back on the joystick, zoomed high into the sky and then shot down towards the bypass. Below him he saw the red tiles of the supermarket. Carefully, he guided the ship until it was hovering in front of the plate glass window by the checkouts. "Stand by to beam up!" he commanded.

SHOOOOM! A tray of bubble gum appeared in the beam upper chamber.

"Hmmm, this really is a most wonderful material!" cooed the Commander, chewing like mad. "So this is what Earthlings need to exercise their faces. Interesting."

"Now watch," said David. "I will show you our way of making a new world." He blew a large pink bubble. **"Blerg!"** said all the Klergs. That was their way of saying "Wow". They all took some bubble gum and noisily chewed and blew. Meanwhile, David set a course for his school.

He raced the traffic along Arkwright Road, skipping in and out among the buses and cars. He skimmed into Crown Street, over the football pitch, over the wire fence and across the playground. When he was outside his classroom, he switched to reverse thrust and shuddered to a halt. He could see the vivarium clearly through the windows.

SHOOOOOM! Up came a nice fat snail. "I collected this for you

because it is one of Earth's most fabulous creatures," said David.

The Commander was terribly impressed by its propulsion unit.

"Ah, you mean its foot? Yes, it makes its own road," said David. "And drives an armoured ship."

"Ah, he reminds me of our Leader, especially his slime and his lovely eyes on stalks," sighed one of the crew. "How marvellous! **Blerg!**"

"Now, I have one more special thing for you to take with you to Planet Klerg," said David. "In it is the history of all the things that the Earthlings of Elmfield have used for many, many years to keep themselves alive. It will give your Leader much fun to study."

"Ah, more fun! Fun is good!"
burbled the Commander happily.
David pulled hard on the joystick
and the spaceship lurched off to the
west, beyond the bypass and the
factories. It took less than two
seconds before they were hovering
over great ugly heaps of rubbish.

"We call this the town dump,"
David explained.

SHOOOOM! went the beam
upper. All the garbage of a hundred
years and more was sucked on
board the *Earthlife Explorer*, shrunk,
and carefully sealed in spacetubes.

Living On Another Planet

The following Monday when school was over, David strolled across the playground with his hands in his pockets. He saw Mr Giles trotting towards him in his red tracksuit, bouncing a football.

"Hands out of your pockets, lad!" he said. "You're slouching!"

"Sorry, sir," said David.

"You spend too much time with those snails, lad!" he grinned.

"You should get out more, run about a bit, get some exercise. Just smell the lovely air! I bet you haven't even noticed that the Council got rid of that dreadful dump at last."

"It wasn't the Council, sir," muttered David.

"Don't mumble, lad!"

"Sorry, sir. I said, are you feeling better, sir?"

"What are you talking about, lad?"

"Well, you've been . . . away, haven't you, sir?"

"Just a little bit of a cold, that's all, David. But when you spend your life in the fresh air like me, you soon get over that sort of thing."

"So you don't remember anything . . . weird happening to you, sir?"

"Now David, you're getting carried away. You want to watch that."

"So you didn't, then, sir?"

Mr Giles opened his mouth to reply but a shout from the Lollipop Lady interrupted him.

"HOY! SLOWCOACH! ARE YOU GONNA CROSS THIS ROAD TODAY OR HAVE I GOT TO HOLD THE TRAFFIC UP TILL WEDNESDAY?"

"Sorry," said David.

"HONESTLY, MR GILES, SOME OF THESE KIDS, IT'S LIKE THEY'RE ON A DIFFERENT PLANET."

"I know exactly what you mean," called Mr Giles.

David smiled to himself and broke into a trot. It was time to take his dear old Hairy Spice for a walk. Then he'd pop along to Arkwright Road and see whether his dad's business had picked up. He hoped so; there was a new computer game he fancied. It was called *Space Rescue II*. David reckoned he might be good at that!